SARAH HUGHES

America's sweetheart

Going for the
GOLD

SARAH HUGHES
America's sweetheart

R.S. Ashby

AVON BOOKS
An Imprint of HarperCollins*Publishers*

For information address
HarperCollins Children's Books, a division of
HarperCollins Publishers, 1350 Avenue of the Americas,
New York, NY 10019.

 Produced by 17th Street Productions,
an Alloy, Inc. company
151 West 26th Street, New York, NY 10001

Library of Congress Catalog Card Number: 2002091350
ISBN 0-06-051842-1

First Avon edition, 2002

AVON TRADEMARK REG. U.S. PAT. OFF.
AND IN OTHER COUNTRIES,
MARCA REGISTRADA, HECHO EN U.S.A.

Visit us on the World Wide Web!
www.harperchildrens.com

For Becky, Sarah, Jessie, Kathryn, and every other girl with a dream

Contents

INTRODUCTION:

Hometown Hero

"I see her! I see Sarah!"

A girl in a pink jacket jumped up and down in excitement. She was standing along a parade route trying to catch a glimpse of her hero, Sarah Hughes—and there she was, coming down the street!

It was March 10, 2002, Sarah Hughes Day in Great Neck, Long Island. Sixteen-year-old Sarah Hughes had just won the Olympic gold medal in women's figure skating, and the town was throwing her a big welcome-home party.

Gold ribbons and bows fluttered along the town's main street. Arches of golden balloons rose into the sky. Mannequins in store windows wore gold medals around their necks. American flags flew everywhere.

Store windows displayed handmade signs: CON-GRATULATIONS SARAH AND FAMILY FROM GINO'S PIZZA! CONGRATULATIONS GOLDEN SARAH FROM THE PERSIAN COMMUNITY OF GREAT NECK! TEMPLE EMANUEL WELCOMES SARAH!

A guy in a red suit and white beard held up his own poster: SANTA LOVES SARAH. Everyone, it seemed, had a special message to send.

The owners of Sarah's favorite neighborhood delicatessen, the Deli on the Green, made a display of her name spelled out in submarine sandwiches, and prepared a bouquet of gold roses just for Sarah.

More than 60,000 people had gathered on this crisp windy day to show their love and pride. This wasn't just any sports star. This was their Sarah, who grew up in *their* town and went to *their* high school. And now the kid who'd started her career at the local ice rink had gone and beaten the best figure skaters in the world. And not at just any old competition. At the most prestigious sporting event of all— the Olympics.

In an interview with a reporter, one friend shared how "it's been really special to see [Sarah] develop from when she was young and [the Olympics were] just a dream, and a goal."

Now the high school band was marching down the street. Sirens blared, and firemen waved at the crowd. Riding in a big cream-colored vintage Thunderbird, New York Senator Hillary Clinton smiled her biggest smile. Senator Chuck Schumer followed, waving enthusiastically.

A Zamboni zigzagged down the middle of the street.

And there—weren't those Sarah's brothers and sisters in that convertible? They looked just like her! "Congratulations!" the crowd yelled, shaking their gold pom-poms.

But where was the champion herself? "Sa-rah! Sa-rah!" people started to chant.

Finally the big moment arrived. Wearing a bright red coat and her giant gold Olympic medal, Sarah Hughes came into view. She was sitting on the backseat of a black Bentley with her coach, Robin Wagner, and her mom and dad, John and Amy Hughes.

Waving and laughing, Sarah was having a wonderful time. Her trademark winning smile was broader than ever. She was so happy to share her victory with all her friends and family, who she described as "all those people who I've known for years and with whom I've always shared my dreams and my goals and my skating."

To Sarah, the past two weeks had been just like a dream. She still had to pinch herself to make sure it was all really true.

"It's the greatest time in my life," she told reporters. "So far. I can't believe so many people watched me skate and shared the enjoyment I went through and so many emotions. I was happy to share it."

What was really amazing was how she had suddenly become a role model for so many kids across the country. "People say, 'I want to be just like you,'" Sarah said in disbelief. "I never thought anyone would want to be just like me."

But they do. At the rink in New Jersey where she trained, Sarah wannabes announced that they, too, long to go to the Olympics someday. A sixteen-year-old said, "It really paid off, all her hard work. That is the lesson for all of us." A thirteen-year-old skater on Long Island commented, "This has taught me to always stay confident and do your best no matter what."

But it isn't just skaters who look to Sarah for inspiration. Everyone, young and old, believes her story has a special meaning for them. A twelve-year-old from Sarah's hometown summed it up: "It makes you feel like you can follow your dream, and you can win, too."

Sarah Hughes, all-American hero, has seen her dream come true. How did she do it? How did she become the Golden Girl?

CHAPTER
ONE:

Born to Skate

It all started with a little girl in a yellow snow-suit. She was three years old, and she wanted to ice skate more than anything in the world. She took a few steps and *splat!* down she fell. Determined, she got up and tried again. *Splat!* She gave a big grin. Already, Sarah Elizabeth Hughes loved the ice.

She was born on May 2, 1985, in the town of Great Neck, Long Island. Sarah was the fourth of six children, two boys and four girls. Her parents, John and Amy Hughes, had always wanted a big family. When he was a boy in Toronto, Canada, John's parents used to care for foster babies. John got used to having lots of kids—and toys and diapers—around. Home wouldn't be home without plenty of children.

So first there was Rebecca, then David, then Matt, Sarah, Emily, and Taylor. The future Olympian grew up in a very full and busy house.

From the beginning, the Hughes children were expected to excel in athletics *and* academics, just as their parents had. John and Amy met at Cornell University in Ithaca, New York, where John was captain of the ice hockey team. In 1970 the team won the national championship, and John thought about going pro. But when he didn't make the final cut for the Toronto Maple Leafs, he went on to law school instead. Amy, meanwhile, went to graduate school for accounting.

But John Hughes hadn't lost his love of hockey. So when the growing family moved to a big split-level home in Great Neck, he built a hockey rink in the backyard. He wanted his kids to enjoy pick-up hockey games whenever they wanted, just as he had growing up in Canada.

"It wasn't a great rink," Sarah told Long Island daily *Newsday* years later. "The ice was bumpy. There was some wiring underneath and, for a little bit, we had a Zamboni. But it broke down, and my dad stayed up all night hosing the ice down."

Her oldest brother, David, who had already had some figure skating lessons, took to hockey immediately. So did his tag-along pal, Matt. But hockey wasn't Sarah's thing. "My mom bought me a pair of hockey skates at one point, but I don't think I ever played," Sarah remembers. The flying pucks scared her. And besides, she didn't want to be on the ice with a bunch of other pushy guys in uniforms and helmets.

She wanted to skate alone!

Already Sarah wanted to be noticed, to be the best. "I was always the one who demanded attention," Sarah told *The New York Times*. "I was always very competitive, regardless of what it was. I tried to skate faster than [my brothers and sisters]. I always wanted to be the first to do everything."

Luckily, there was a big local rink nearby. Sarah used to go along with her older siblings when they went for lessons and practice. The kids would sit on the bench to wait for their mother to tie their skates. Once, because Sarah was so impatient, Amy did hers first. As soon as she was finished, Sarah flew off the bench and onto the ice. Frantic, her mother had to call out to the attendants to catch the little girl before someone crashed into her.

Next time, her mother put Sarah's skates on last. But Sarah couldn't stand to wait. So at age three, Sarah learned to tie her laces herself!

"It wasn't so important for me to tie my skates first," Sarah remembers. "It was because I was the only one who could do it right, how *I* liked it."

Sarah can barely recall when she started skating. "I remember being really young and taking group skating," she told *Newsday*. "We played red light, green light. The instructor was at one end, and whoever reached the other end won."

Others remember how happy the toddler always seemed on the ice. When her first coach, Patti Johnson, first saw Sarah she was wearing molded plastic skates. "She got on the ice, and she ran and fell and giggled and got up and ran again," Johnson told *Newsday*. "She had no fear."

Sarah took to the ice like a duck to water. In fact, she was a prodigy. She soon mastered moves it took other children many years to learn. Figure skating is a complicated and difficult art. It requires many years of dedicated training.

Skating itself is probably four thousand years old. People in Northern Europe, who needed to be able to get around on ice in cold weather, made crude skates out of animal bones. They tied the bones around their feet with leather thongs. The blades were usually made of reindeer, elk, or horse bones. But some were made of walrus tusks!

Skating was good transportation. Soon people discovered it was fun, too. By the 1400s, the Dutch had invented iron skates for use on their frozen canals. The rest is sports history.

Gradually blades got narrower and sharper. Today's blades are made of polished steel. The bottom of the blade has a slight inward curve to it, with a groove down the middle. The groove gives the blade a sharp edge on each side. On the tip of the blade is the "toe pick," five sharp points that dig into the ice. The edges and the toe pick allow skaters to turn, jump, and spin.

With advances in design, skating became easier and more enjoyable. By the 1860s, skating was all the rage, especially in the United States. One of the great things about ice skating was that it was a sport women could enjoy, too.

Women became great skaters. It was a good omen for the future!

As blades became more flexible, people started to add fancy jumps and spins to show off their skill. As they did, figure skating developed. Figure skating gets its name from the patterns, or figures, that people learned to trace on the ice with the edge of their blades. For a long time all competitions included what were called "compulsory" figures as well as "free skating." The figures were intricate and inventive—swirls, flowers, or arabesques. You won't see compulsory figures in competitions anymore, though. They aren't as athletically challenging or fun to watch as jumps or spins. Figures were finally dropped from international competition in 1990.

The first thing three-year-old Sarah needed to know in order to figure skate was how to glide without falling over. First she would push off using a T-push. That means she arranged her feet like a *T* and pushed with her back foot. Into a glide she went, moving smoothly across the ice. She raised one foot off the ice, then the other. She was still standing upright! And before she knew it, she was "stroking" like a real pro.

With each stroke, she would push off to the side and backward with the edge of her blade. It is important to figure skate on edge. That way you can go in a circle or curve. Sarah spent hours practicing gliding on the outside edge, then on the inside edge. Soon she could go faster and faster. She'd need both speed and sureness on edge to be able to do jumps and spins someday.

In no time at all, Sarah was zipping across the ice. But if she wanted to be a good figure skater, she didn't just need to move fast. She needed to move gracefully. That was where the ballet lessons came in.

From age three to fourteen, Sarah took ballet lessons twice a week. At the Great Neck School of Dance she learned the basic moves of ballet—the port de bras, the pirouette, the arabesque, and more. Someday she would put these moves together with her spins and jumps into a beautiful cohesive program.

Her former dance teacher Roberta Senn is adamant about the importance of ballet. "Figure skaters—the best skaters—must also be ballet dancers," she told *Newsday*. Sarah was such an excellent dancer that Senn begged her to continue. But Sarah had her eyes on the prize—in skating. So by the time Sarah was a teenager and her teacher suggested she go *en pointe*, on her toes, she and her family decided against it. It might hurt her feet for skating, so that was that.

By the time Sarah was five, all she knew was that she wanted to keep skating forever. Soon word got around the New York skating community that this energetic youngster had something special. She started being invited to skate in ice shows and exhibitions. When she was six, she traveled upstate to Lake Placid and shared the spotlight at an exhibition with Kristi Yamaguchi. Yamaguchi had just won the gold medal at the 1992 Olympics.

Sarah had actually watched Kristi win that gold. It was her first memory of seeing the Olympics on TV. And now Sarah got to meet her hero in person!

John Hughes looked on as his daughter performed in front of thousands of people. He was amazed to see how self-assured and happy she seemed.

"I was sitting there, watching Sarah in the spotlight," he told *U.S. Figure Skating Online*. "All the people around me had paid a lot of money to see this, and there's my daughter down on the ice! Sarah didn't let anything get to her. That's when I felt this was something she was going to do."

The spotlight was just where Sarah wanted to be. "I love to perform," Sarah has confessed. "I love to be onstage and have people watch me skate. I enjoy being the center of attention."

Soon younger sister Emily caught the skating bug, too. A few years later, both were invited to skate at the opening of the Rockefeller Center skating rink. They chatted with TV star Kathie Lee Gifford on one of her Christmas specials. Sarah even did a European tour with famous Russian coach Natalia Dubova and the world ice dance champions.

The starstruck girl became friends with skating champions Scott Hamilton, men's gold medal winner in 1984, JoJo Starbuck, U.S. pairs champion in the 1970s, and Peggy Fleming, ladies' Olympic gold medal winner in 1968.

It was heady stuff for an eight-year-old. But Sarah's family kept her feet on the ground, even when her head was in the clouds.

After all, Sarah wasn't an only child, the sole focus of her parents' attention. She was one of six. In the Hughes family, every child was special. The household was always a whirlwind of activity. There was older sister Rebecca, a super student who loved to read and write. She was a figure skater, too, until she reached fifteen and turned her attention to editing her newspaper at Great Neck North High.

David played hockey in high school, too, and led his team to two state championships. Matt played not only hockey but golf and tennis, at a nearby private school with smaller classes. Emily followed Sarah into skating, entering competitions and performing in exhibitions.

And Taylor, the baby of the family? Like her oldest sister Rebecca, she turned out to be an avid reader and Scrabble player. Taylor also loves acting and—not surprisingly—figure skating and hockey.

"What's really been good with all our kids," John Hughes told *Newsday*, "is that they all seem to have found something that they're very happy to do."

In this happy, busy family there was Sarah, skating away. She was so obsessed she even used to go to school in her skating dresses. (By the time she got to high school, she says, she had learned that skating dresses were very uncool!)

Sarah knew just what she wanted to do that year, and the next, and the next after that. In a home movie taken when she was about eight, she laid it all out.

"I want to be in the Olympics and get a gold medal," Sarah Hughes said, looking straight into the camera. "I can't wait for that to happen."

CHAPTER
TWO:

Rising Star

So Sarah Hughes wanted to go to the Olympics, and when she grew up, she just went. End of story.

Isn't that the way it happens?

Nope.

It is a long, hard road to the Olympics. Every eight-year-old skater in the country can picture herself on the medals podium. But very few—just a handful—actually make it. What separates the winners from the wannabes?

A combination of luck, pluck, and skill. An iron will to succeed. And unswerving determination.

Sarah has always been lucky in that she has a loving, supportive, achievement-oriented family.

She has an upbeat, optimistic nature—"a

great inner spirit," as her first coach has said. "It's just a twinkle and a sparkle that you can't explain."

She is a great natural athlete. By age five, Sarah could already make jumps and spins that kids much older than she couldn't do.

She is extremely competitive. For as long as she can remember, Sarah has always had the will to win. And the tougher the competition the harder she works—and the better she does.

And, as we have seen, she really, really wanted to get to the Olympics.

But every big goal requires a succession of smaller achievements along the way. Step by step, Sarah advanced down the path she had chosen for herself. For thirteen years she pushed herself to the limit, learning and perfecting her skills. She got out on the ice—every single day. And she sweated.

Finally she reached her goal.

Here's how she did it.

If you've ever watched a world-class figure skater on TV or in a rink, you know that their movements look joyous and natural. The better they are the more effortless their skating seems. But what seems like free expression is really art.

Each "spontaneous" move is carefully choreographed. Each jump and spin and spiral is compulsory, or required. Routines performed at competitions each contain a certain number of required moves. Skaters must execute them correctly, or they don't count. Sure there's room for individual creativity, but only after the basic standards have been met. There's no use creating an innovative jump if a skater can't do a standard triple toe loop.

Like every young skater, Sarah Hughes faced the challenge of learning a whole vocabulary of moves. Some were relatively easy. Some were very tough! Here are some of the most important:

SPIRAL: A glide in an arc while extending one leg behind at hip level or higher. The spiral is based on the ballet arabesque position and can be breathtakingly beautiful. Sarah's ballet lessons came in handy when she learned the spiral.

SPIN: A twirl performed at a really high speed. Some of the best known include:
- **Scratch spin** A spin on two legs, done with the arms held close to the body.

Skaters can accelerate rapidly on this spin. You know those spins in which the performer twirls so rapidly she becomes a blur? Those are scratch spins. They often provide a dramatic ending to a program.

- **Sit spin** A spin done in a sitting position. One knee is bent, and the other leg is extended.
- **Camel spin** An upright spin on one leg in which the other leg is extended in a position parallel to the ice.
- **Layback** A spin on one leg in which the head, shoulders, and back are arched backward. The other leg is held in a ballet "attitude" position. This is mainly performed by women and requires a very flexible body. Not surprisingly, Sarah is especially good at it.

JUMP: A leap into the air. There are two types of jumps: edge takeoff jumps, and toe pick-assisted jumps. The best way to tell individual jumps apart is by their different takeoffs and landings. Once the skater is rotating in the air, double and triple jumps look the same. The axel is the only jump approached from a forward position. The lutz requires a long backward glide, usually into a corner of the rink. And so on.

- **Waltz** An edge jump with a half revolution into the air. The simplest jump, the waltz is the one Sarah probably learned first.
- **Salchow** An edge jump that takes off from the back inside edge of one foot and ends on the back outside edge of the other. It is named for its inventor, Ulrich Salchow, a Swedish skating sensation from the early 1900s. (I bet you've always wondered where the strange name came from!)
- **Toe loop** A toe-pick jump that starts and lands on the same back outside edge.
- **Split** A toe-pick jump in which the legs split apart, the body leans forward, and the hands touch the toes of the boots.
- **Loop** An edge jump that takes off and lands on the same backside edge.
- **Flip** A toe-pick jump that starts from the back inside edge of one foot and ends on the back outside edge of the opposite foot.
- **Lutz** A toe-pick jump that starts from the back outside edge of one foot and lands on the back outside edge of the other foot. It is named after its creator, Alois Lutz.

- **Axel** An edge jump that starts from the forward outside edge of one foot and finishes on the back outside edge of the opposite foot. This is the hardest jump to learn—a single axel is just the beginning. A double axel has two and a half revolutions, and a triple axel has three and a half revolutions! It is named for its inventor, Axel Paulsen. It took Sarah more than two years to learn to do a double axel.

As the bar has been raised higher in figure skating, athletes are performing more and harder jumps. In the first decade of the 21st century, combination jumps are all-important—two or more jumps linked together with no steps in between. You'll hear commentators refer to a triple toe-triple toe, or a triple lutz-double loop.

Quadruple jumps, or "quads," are practically mandatory for men today who want to make it to the elite levels of skating. But no woman has ever nailed a quad in competition—though some are working on it.

When Sarah was learning how to skate, the most difficult jump a woman had ever managed in competition was the triple axel. (If a jump isn't done in competition, it's not official, according to international skating rules.) Japan's Midori Ito caused a sensation when she landed a triple axel at the World Championships in 1989. And America's Tonya Harding managed one at both the 1991 U.S. National Figure Skating Championships and the 1991 World Figure Skating Championships. But as of 2002, no American woman had landed one in ten years.

When she was a young girl, a triple or even a double axel was far in Sarah's future. In the beginning, she needed to concentrate on the basic jumps. She quickly showed herself to be a jumping whiz. By age five, Sarah could already do double toe loops and double salchows. Her parents treasure a picture of Sarah at six, up in the air and touching her toes in a perfect split. Her face is serious, her hair is flying, and she's having a great time.

In order to advance as a figure skater, Sarah needed to compete. And in order to compete, she had to join a local skating club and follow the guidelines for competitive skating laid out by the United States Figure Skating Association. The USFSA regulates competitive skating in the United States.

There are eight levels of proficiency: Pre-Preliminary, Preliminary, Pre-Juvenile, Juvenile,

Intermediate, Novice, Junior, and Senior. The levels are determined not by age but by expertise. In order to advance up the ladder, skaters have to take two tests in front of a judge. If they pass, they can move to the next level.

When Sarah started taking lessons at age four, her first Pre-Preliminary test would have required that she do forward stroking and basic edges. The next, or Preliminary, test required three-turns, spirals, and crossovers. Sarah moved through the earliest levels so quickly that by the time she was eight, she was ready for the Novice level.

In the summer of 1994, her local skating magazine, *As the Rink Turns*, raved: "One of the rising stars is eight-year-old Sarah Hughes. She may attain Novice Lady ranking this year. That level is usually attained by girls between 13-15 years old." The article ran next to a picture of a beaming Sarah posed with Olympic bronze medal winner Nancy Kerrigan at Lake Placid.

Sarah had been working with coach Patti Johnson since she was four. When she was nine, after she became a Novice, she added another member to her team, choreographer Robin Wagner. As choreographer, Wagner put all of

Sarah's required moves together into a balanced routine.

Wagner, who had studied skating herself, was doing the choreography for about thirty other students at the time. But immediately she noticed that Sarah was something special. For one thing, she had phenomenal jumping ability (no matter how long it took her to do a double axel!). Still, she was a challenge to the choreographer. "She just wanted to jump around," Wagner told *Newsday*. "She didn't want to pay attention to her hands and her arms."

Sarah would have to pay attention to every element of skating when she went to her first Novice competition in 1996. Novices are the first level of skaters allowed to compete in the U.S. National Championships, held every year in January. In order to qualify for the Nationals, Sarah first had to enter the Regionals. Coming from Long Island, her region was the North Atlantic Region, comprising New York and New Jersey, and Erie, Pennsylvania.

That year, when Sarah was ten, she went to her first major competition. She was determined to win. And she came in third!

That qualified her to move on to the Eastern

Sectional. But there she only came in tenth. There would be no Nationals for her in 1996.

No matter. She would try again in 1997.

The next year, Sarah won a gold medal at the North Atlantic Regional competition. But she still didn't make it all the way to the Nationals. Instead, the National Novice gold medal was won by a Korean-American girl named Naomi Nari Nam. Sarah would be seeing lots of Naomi in the next few years.

Now Sarah had a big decision to make. Should she stay in Novice or move up to Junior? She knew she had all the moves to be a Junior. But she might have a better chance of winning a medal at the Novice level. Sarah discussed the decision with her coach, her choreographer, and her parents. Together, they decided Sarah was ready for the challenge. At age twelve she would become a Junior, the second-highest level in ladies' figure skating.

Sarah could hardly wait for the Nationals.

In the meantime, Sarah was growing up. She entered middle school, got braces, and grew her hair out. Usually she pulled her long brown hair back into a ponytail, which swung behind her head as she skated.

In some ways Sarah was a typical twelve-year-old. She loved her school classes, especially math and science. She enjoyed being with friends and adored her family. She loved palling around with their golden retriever named Sport (what else!).

She helped make breakfast for her family every morning and learned to do her own laundry. As she got older, she sometimes baby-sat for her younger sisters. Her mother wanted Sarah to have the kinds of experiences most girls have. As Amy Hughes told *The New York Times*, "I've always said my job is really to keep her as normal as possible."

Most of Sarah's time, though, was taken up with skating. Like most young figure skaters, Sarah skated before school and after school every day, all year, year after year. She needed as much private time on the ice as she could get, because figure skaters need a lot of room to practice. They can't do flips and lutzes when other people are on the ice; someone could get hurt. So Sarah would get up at four or five o'clock just to have the ice to herself.

It's tough to have the discipline to get up so early. As Sarah confessed to Katie Couric on *The Today Show*, "It's really difficult. Some days you're like, Ugh, I just want to stay in bed all day."

But Sarah knew what she wanted to achieve, so she kept at it. Besides, even if she did have to travel to get to an ice rink, it was worth it to live with her family in her own hometown. Lots of young figure skaters decide to move away in order to train with an internationally known trainer. 1998 Olympic gold medalist Tara Lipinski, for instance, moved all over the country with her mother in order to work with the right coaches. While they lived in Delaware and Detroit, her father stayed in Texas to work and pay the bills. Michelle Kwan and her mother also left home so Michelle could train at the famous Ice Castle in Lake Arrowhead, California.

But Sarah didn't want to leave home. She wanted to stay right where she was—with all her brothers and sisters. With hard work, dedication, and lots of love, they would make it all work somehow.

That year she would be happier than ever she decided to stay home.

In 1997 Sarah should have been on top of the world. She was working hard, skating better all the time, and could look forward to an exciting year competing in the Juniors for the very first time.

But then the unthinkable happened. Her mother got sick. Very sick.

Amy Hughes had breast cancer. Cancer is a very serious disease that occurs when tissue starts to grow unnaturally fast. When it is caught early enough and the whole tumor is removed or shrunk, people usually recover. But if the cancer cells have already traveled into the bloodstream and the cancer has spread, or metastasized, it can be deadly.

Amy would have to have surgery, and then chemotherapy afterward. Chemotherapy is supposed to kill whatever cancer cells still survive after the surgery. In the face of this emergency, the whole family pitched in to support Amy and help each other. Rebecca, who was already at Harvard, flew down each weekend to take care of the youngest girls, Emily and Taylor. David donated his blood to help his mother recover from the chemotherapy.

At twelve Sarah was old enough to understand what was happening. She was worried for her mother but also hopeful that she would recover. After all, everyone in the skating world knew the inspiring story of Scott Hamilton. He got testicular cancer, was treated, and lived. If Scott could survive, her mother would, too.

She told her mother everything would be fine. "I wanted to call up Scott Hamilton and just kiss him," Amy wrote on *U.S. Figure Skating Online*. "Someone my daughter knew of and admired so much had been through cancer and beat it."

Meanwhile, Sarah knew that the best way to help her mother was by continuing to skate. If she worked hard, her mother would, too. They would fight—and win—together.

So that fall a very determined Sarah won the North Atlantic Junior Regional Championships. Then the Eastern Junior Sectionals. Finally she had earned a ticket to the Nationals!

The only drawback was that her mother, ill in New York, wouldn't be able to make it all the way to Philadelphia to see her skate. But to Sarah's amazement, Amy willed herself to get out of bed. When Sarah skated the long program at the National Championships, her mother was sitting in the stands, watching.

And she saw her daughter climb the podium to claim her prize—the gold medal at the 1998 Junior National Championships!

Sarah had won!

Back home in Great Neck, the town threw her a party. "We celebrated the victory of our Sarah, who has been skating since she was three years old," said Richard Arenella, who was at the time superintendent of the Great Neck Parks and Recreation Department. He pointed proudly to a banner that had been hung in her honor. "We hope it will still be hanging four years from now when Sarah wins gold at the Salt Lake City Olympics!"

Best of all, Sarah knew that her effort had helped her mother. Watching Sarah skate made her feel so good that Amy began to call her "Dr. Sarah."

Finally Amy Hughes's cancer went into remission. Amy was no longer a cancer patient—she was a cancer survivor. Sarah and her mother had won together after all!

Now that Sarah's full focus was back on her skating, another important change was in store for her. Sarah had had the same coach since she was four years old. Now she was ready for the big time, and her parents were ready for a change.

They decided to ask her choreographer, Robin Wagner, to be her coach, too. It was a bold move. Robin wasn't an internationally known skating coach. In fact, she'd never coached anyone at the elite level before. But John and Amy Hughes had been watching Robin carefully. They could see her energy, her expertise, her intelligence. The petite, pretty Robin was a human dynamo and an organizational fiend. They knew she could manage the complicated scheduling, the press, the clothes, and the makeup as well as the double axels and toe loops. Just as important, they saw how well she related to Sarah.

Robin Wagner, they decided, had what it took to get Sarah to the very top.

Growing up in Hewlett Harbor, Long Island, Robin also wanted to be a skating star. Driven and competitive, she pushed herself to succeed. In high school, her crazy schedule mirrored Sarah's years later: Up at 4 A.M. to take skating lessons in Manhattan. Back to the island by 10 A.M. for school. Ballet lessons. Piano lessons. Studying.

Robin actually made it to the Junior Nationals twice. Once she came in fifth. But by the time she graduated from prestigious Barnard College, Robin had given up competitive skating. Instead, over the years, she took on a variety of roles. She worked in the production department of her father's trade news publication. She taught skating. She became an assistant buyer at tony New York department store Bergdorf Goodman. Always she drifted back to her first love, skating.

By the time Sarah met her in 1995, Robin had taught herself choreography. If she took on Sarah full time, she'd be able to put it all together: the choreography, the music, the fashion, the skating. The Hugheses had offered Robin the opportunity of a lifetime: the chance to mold someone into an Olympic skater. If she succeeded, it would make Robin's reputation as well as Sarah's.

Of course Robin jumped at the offer. Sarah couldn't have been more thrilled. As far as she was concerned, Robin was cool. "She was always asking me whether I like something," Sarah told *Time*. "When you're ten, you always want to be the boss, and when someone asks you for your input, you get really excited."

Together, they would do great things!

Chapter

Three:

A Skater's Life

Sarah was the national junior ladies' champion. So she was poised to become senior national, world, and Olympic champion, too. Right?

Wrong. There was the small matter of the "junior title curse." Of all the junior champions since 1986, only one had ever made it to the Olympics, and she was a pairs skater.

This isn't because all those dedicated champions suddenly lose the will to win. It's because their bodies are taken over by an alien force—hormones. Between the ages of ten and fifteen, young girls grow into women. Their bodies go crazy, growing up and sideways all at once. Short girls may shoot into beanpoles. Small girls grow hips.

With every growth spurt, the body's balance

shifts. Skaters who rely on their bodies to act a certain way when they do a familiar jump suddenly have to learn the jump all over again. Their balance is off.

Adolescence is an exciting and confusing time for all girls. There are all the normal distractions of being a teenager—clothes, makeup, friends, school, and boys. But elite skaters like Sarah have an added challenge. When Sarah won the Juniors, she found herself in the national spotlight. Suddenly she had press interviews. Fans. Web sites. People she didn't even know were discussing her looks, her clothes, her body. It's tough to grow up in the public eye and keep your self-esteem.

Robin took it upon herself to monitor the Web sites. As she told *Newsday*, she knew that Sarah would hear that she was "gawky, awkward, had poor posture, lack of maturity. But at twelve or thirteen you're supposed to be gawky and awkward. It's perfectly natural." Somehow, Robin would protect her from as many comments as possible.

She was determined that Sarah would get through the next few years with her self-esteem and skating ability intact.

*   *   *

The offers started to pour in. Sarah was invited to skate on the Junior Grand Prix circuit, a series of international competitions. The Hungarian trophy in Budapest. The Mexico Cup in Mexico City. And then the World Junior Figure Skating Championships in Zagreb, Croatia. She was only in eighth grade, and already she was seeing the world.

Sarah came away from the year with a handful of silver medals and a question. She'd done everything she could on the Junior circuit. Was it time to try Senior?

The Senior level was where all the stars were. 1996 European champion Irina Slutskaya. 1999 world champion Maria Butyrskaya. And 1998 Olympic silver medalist Michelle Kwan.

Did thirteen-year-old Sarah have what it took to compete at that level? She had already mastered all five triple jumps used by the best women skaters. But still . . .

There was only one way to find out.

The 1999 National Championships took place at the Delta Center in Salt Lake City, Utah. That's where the Winter Olympic Games would be held in just three years. Sarah hoped it was a good sign!

She walked into the championships starstruck. Everyone she had admired for so long was there. But Sarah couldn't allow herself to be overwhelmed. She had work to do.

There are two parts to any National, World, or Olympic competition: the short program and the long program. The short program is two minutes and forty seconds long and contains eight required elements. Missing or messing up on any of these required elements means a mandatory reduction in the judges' marks. The short program counts for one-third of the final score.

The long, or free skate, program accounts for the other two-thirds. At four minutes, it draws on every jumping, spinning, and footwork skill the skater has. Although the long program has no required elements, judges award higher marks for more difficult moves. So it pays to take chances.

In both the long and short programs, skaters are allowed to choose their own music, costumes, and choreography. It is up to them to create their own personality and presence on the ice.

Sarah, at thirteen, wasn't going to choose too sophisticated an outfit, or music that emphasized passion and maturity. "It's a fine line," Sarah explained to the Augusta *Chronicle*. "You try to be yourself, but you don't want to skate like a child, either. I don't want to act fifteen or twenty."

The solution for Robin and Sarah was to have Sarah skate to Chopin's "Fantasie-Impromptu" for the short program and Tchaikovsky's *Swan Lake* for the long. Both pieces are lovely, lyrical, and familiar.

When Sarah stepped onto the ice for the short program, she was wearing a simple peach-colored costume with sequins along the neckline. Her long hair was pulled back with a peach scrunchy.

And then Sarah soared. She sailed through all her jumps, and whirled through her spins. The judges were impressed. Here was a girl who knew exactly what she was doing—and could do it under pressure. They awarded her very high marks.

Sarah was ecstatic. Not only had she skated her best, but she was in second place—just behind Michelle Kwan!

"It's so exciting," Sarah exclaimed to reporters afterward. "I'm so happy I'm here this year. I'm happy that I skated well, and I'm really pleased to be in second place."

But it was the long program that would determine whether she'd win a medal. Sarah performed her *Swan Lake* routine in a white dress decorated with sparkling beads. This time she wore her hair pinned up in a ballerina's bun.

The first lush chords sounded, and Sarah prepared for her opening triple jump. She was up in the air, rotating—

And then, as she tried to land, it happened.

She fell!

Sarah felt her heart drop. But now was no time to panic. People fell all the time in competitions. The main thing was to keep going. And keep smiling!

She nailed a triple lutz. But then, in a second lutz-double toe loop combination, she fell again.

Again Sarah picked herself up and continued. Then she steeled herself for her final jump. It was a triple toe-triple toe combination. It was so hard that up until then only 1998 Olympic gold medalist Tara Lipinski had ever landed one in national competition.

And she did it!

Sarah was happy to come back after her mistakes. That was what the real pros did. But it didn't look as if she'd win a medal at these nationals after all.

Well, she did win a medal—sort of. She won the little-known "pewter" for a fourth-place finish. Michelle Kwan took the gold.

But there was another surprise in store for Sarah. It turned out that the second-place finisher, Naomi Nari Nam, was thirteen and still too young to go to the Worlds. Sarah was also officially too young, but according to an obscure World Championships rule, if someone medals at the Junior World Championships, she is eligible for Senior Worlds no matter what her age. And Sarah had won silver that year in Juniors, so she was able to take Naomi's place at the 1999 World Championships.

Sarah was the youngest woman at the competition. She didn't expect to win a medal. She just wanted to have fun and do her best. And she did. When the event was over, Sarah was ranked seventh—in the world!

It looked as if Sarah might escape the junior champion curse after all. She and Robin settled into a routine that would keep Sarah on top. That fall she would be fourteen and going into high school. She would have a crushing routine of practices, shows, and competitions. She would also have a demanding schedule of homework, papers, and tests. Somehow, she still wanted to squeeze in a life with family and friends.

It was time to get serious!

Sarah was no longer training on her home turf in Great Neck. Since she'd turned twelve, she and Robin had been making a daily commute to the Ice House in Hackensack, New Jersey. The Ice House opened in 1998 for the many top skaters in the New York metropolitan area. With its four-ring complex, it offered skaters like Hughes a lot more private time on the ice than any place on Long Island could.

So six days a week, her mother dropped Sarah off in the local Macy's parking lot, and then Sarah got into Robin's SUV and started the one- to two-hour drive to the rink. On the way, they talked and laughed and caught up on the day—gossip, school, music, jokes, whatever. "Car time is for talking about anything but skating," Robin says.

They started reading the editorial page of *The New York Times* and discussing current events. Sarah discovered that she loved discussing politics—especially with Robin, who always had an opinion!

Next came training for two or three hours at the Ice House. Robin was right on the ice with her, correcting, praising, making suggestions. And more suggestions! Sarah fit in two hours of conditioning, before and after practice. Then it was back in the car for another two-hour commute home.

Two or three times a week, Sarah showed up at a fitness center in Great Neck for a high-intensity workout. Only strong muscles allowed her to make those jumps, and only muscles helped her land them. Then there were hours of massage therapy to keep her body flexible and loose.

As she got older, touring took up more and more of Sarah's time. Competing at the highest level in figure skating meant attending meets around the world. But in between the practices and the championships, Sarah and Robin tried to see the sights, too. Over the years, they attended the Viennese Opera in Vienna and visited the Hermitage Museum in St. Petersburg. They ate sushi in Japan. And they shopped in Paris. Sometimes Sarah's family came to watch her skate, too. Then they would all have a great time together.

Sarah's motto is "work hard and have fun." Somehow, she managed to do both.

How did she find time for school, too? With a lot of juggling! In sixth and seventh grade, Sarah would practice in the mornings and after school. But by eighth grade, she had started taking the long trip to the Ice House. That often left her time for one early morning class at Great Neck North High School every day.

To Sarah and her parents that one class was precious. As her assistant principal put it, Sarah got an hour and a half every day just to be a kid.

John Hughes agrees. "We've been very lucky," he told *Newsday*. "She's getting her training and she's getting educated."

Sarah thought school was cool. "Sometimes it can be really, really stressful," she has admitted. "Like if I have to do an essay. But I really like math and science and I like being able to go to school. When I come back from competitions, kids will say, 'Oh, we saw you on TV and we were all cheering for you.' I feel a whole support system from my school, and that's really nice. I have the best of both worlds."

Around Great Neck North, she was known as "Sarah the Skater."

Since Sarah couldn't always be in school, the

school came to her. Each year, she had a tutor for every subject. She kept in touch with her tutors by phone, by e-mail, and in occasional face-to-face meetings at the local Starbucks or at home. It was up to Sarah to do the reading, write the essays, and take the tests—by herself.

"One-on-one," Sarah told *Newsday*, "it's harder. "You kind of have to do your work."

Luckily, Sarah is an excellent student. It's all because she wants to be a scholar *and* an athlete. "What I feel in Sarah," her history teacher Susan Babkes told *Newsday*, "is the same discipline she has for skating, she has for studies. It's the person she is. She's gifted, she has discipline, and she has focus."

Also, as her math tutor adds, Sarah has an advanced placement in time-management!

Still the competitions kept coming. And with every year, Sarah got a little better. In 2000 she finished third at Nationals, this time behind Michelle Kwan and another up-and-coming star, fifteen-year-old Sasha Cohen. Sasha had the makings of a champion, no doubt about it.

But Sarah was impressive, too. ABC-TV commentator Peggy Fleming noted that "in just twelve short months, Sarah has changed from that awkward thirteen-year-old girl we first saw, and now she is a poised and elegant competitor."

Poised and elegant maybe, but Sarah and Robin felt that something was missing. Maybe a makeover was in order. That's when they decided to make the big move and cut Sarah's hair.

The haircut would be a rite of passage, a message to the world that Sarah was all grown up and ready to be taken seriously. They both knew that it was time Sarah projected a more mature image.

The haircut they chose would be fitting, almost symbolic. It was short and sassy, similar to Dorothy Hamill's wedge cut at the 1976 Olympics. After Hamill won the gold medal, every girl in the country wanted her look.

The new cut framed Sarah's face, emphasizing her bright eyes and broad smile. She went from looking like a little girl to a woman. Almost.

Best of all, she finally got rid of her braces!

It probably wasn't the hair, but Sarah did do extremely well at the World Championships that next month. At the end of the competition, she was ranked fifth in the world.

Slowly but inevitably she was inching her way up the ladder. The next year, in 2001, she was second in the Nationals behind Michelle Kwan and third in the Worlds, behind Michelle and Irina Slutskya. Two medals—a silver and a bronze!

Then the incredible happened—in fall 2001, she beat both Michelle and Irina at an international competition called Skate Canada.

It couldn't have happened at a better time. Just four months away was the event Sarah had been waiting for her whole life—the 2002 Winter Olympics at Salt Lake City. But first came the most important Nationals of her career. Only the three United States medalists would be allowed to represent their country at the Olympics. The previous year, Sarah had won a silver medal. Perhaps this year it would be a gold?

Sarah went to the 2002 U.S. National Championships with high expectations.

But she had forgotten all about Sasha Cohen. Sasha had spent the previous year out of competition with a bad injury. Now she was back and ready to roll.

Sasha charmed the judges with a spectacular routine and beat Sarah to a silver medal, while Michelle Kwan took the gold.

Sarah ended up with a bronze. While it wasn't what she'd hoped for, the medal meant that Sarah would be going to the Olympics, and she was relieved and excited.

But she and Robin both knew that if she wanted an Olympic medal, Sarah would have to go all out. Seize the day. Grab the moment.

Sarah would have to wow the Olympic judges with the best performance of her life.

CHAPTER
FOUR:

The Road To Salt Lake

Sarah and Robin didn't have much time to prepare.

Sarah won the bronze medal at the Nationals on January 12, and February 8 was the day of the opening ceremony for the Olympics.

There was less than a month to devise a plan of action that would give Sarah the best shot possible at the medal she'd dreamed of for years.

Sarah has a classic, elegant presence on the ice. *Time* magazine has called it "Well disciplined and consistent." *Newsweek* said she skates with "confidence and serenity."

Serenity was all very well and good, Sarah thought, but would the Olympic judges really care? They tended to award performers who skated with pizzazz, like 1994 gold medalist

Oksana Baiul and 1998 champion Tara Lipinski.

In order to catch the judges' attention, Sarah would have to have some pizzazz herself. "We both felt, 'You're in the Olympics; there's no reason to play it safe,'" Wagner told *Newsday*.

They started with the music. Robin had talked to a judge at the Nationals who'd thought the music Sarah used in the long program, from Ravel's *Daphnis and Chloë*, was somewhat flat. She wanted to recut the last 90 seconds to end the program with a bang. So they visited an expert music cutter in New Jersey. He chopped off the original Rachmaninoff piano concerto ending and searched *Daphnis and Chloë* for a fitting climax. Now Sarah's program would end with a big, emotional crescendo and a crash of cymbals. The audience would love it.

Robin also rechoreographed the routine to fit the music, and Sarah learned the new routine in record time.

Then there was Sarah's hair. For the past ten years, her hair had been cut by the same hairdresser on Long Island. The look was young and bouncy. The time was ripe, she felt, for something different. So off she went to the Elizabeth Arden salon in Manhattan, where celebrity hairdresser Vincent Roppatte gave her a new do. The result was shorter, lighter, more sophisticated. Sarah complained that it was *too* short, but Robin assured her it would grow out in time for the Olympics. It did.

Next they had to consider clothes. Costume is absolutely key to the impression a skater makes on the audience and on the judges. Olympic costumes, especially, tend to linger in the mind. They can help make a skater a legend.

Everyone of a certain age can remember the flowing lime-green dress Peggy Fleming wore in the 1968 Olympics. Her mother made it, as she did all of Peggy's costumes. Dorothy Hamill wore a rich dark pink in 1976, perfect for her fresh, all-American good looks. That dress was homemade, too, and cost only seventy-five dollars!

The marvelous Katerina Witt glowed in a frothy peasant dress in 1984. And how about Nancy Kerrigan's sparkling champagne dress in 1992, decorated with more than five thousand sequins? That was the inspiration of bridal designer Vera Wang. Kerrigan and Wang started a whole new trend in designer Olympic costumes.

The days of handsewn dresses were definitely over. Sarah had always gotten her costumes from Tania Bass, a designer in New York City. Bass had made some beautiful outfits over the years, including the sand-colored number Sarah wore at the 2000 World Championships and the black-and-red stunner she wore for her *Don Quixote* skate in the 2001 World Championships. But just as Robin had changed Sarah's music, choreography, and haircut, she also felt that a new style of costume could help set this performance apart from any in Sarah's past. So Robin contacted Los Angeles-based designer Jef Billings, who has designed costumes for the touring show Stars on Ice. She faxed Billings Sarah's measurements and begged him to make two dresses on short notice. According to Robin, an Olympic dress should be "wow!"

Billings quickly drew up some sketches. For the short program, he promised something with an "ecclesiastical (churchlike) feel." Sarah would be skating the program to Gounod's "Ave Maria." For the long program he suggested a "crisp pastel."

Sarah wouldn't even be able to try on the outfits until she arrived in Salt Lake City. She and

Robin prayed the last-minute rush would be worth it.

Bass, meanwhile, would be shipping two new creations for the practices. Sarah would have a total of four new dresses for the Olympics.

Then, most important, Sarah and Robin had to fine-tune Sarah's skating. Especially her lutz.

The triple lutz is one of the most difficult jumps a woman skater can make. Only the triple axel is tougher. Sarah would take off on the back outside edge of one foot and land on the back outside edge of the other. But like many women skaters, she tended to fudge it, landing a "flutz." She kept slipping onto the inside edge before taking off. The move requires that the upper body rotate in an opposite direction from the hips on takeoff. Many women lack the upper-body strength to counter the rotation.

The fault might be common, Sarah knew, but it could have serious consequences. Judges would take off valuable points for a flutz. She had been trying to relearn the jump for three months. All she could do was keep on practicing.

There was an added complication. Sarah performs her jumps in the opposite direction from most skaters. She spins clockwise instead of counterclockwise. That means that she sets her jumps up from a different direction, too. Up until now she had been performing her imperfect lutz in the corner of the rink where the TV cameras were set up. That meant judges could see mistakes clearly in a replay. Just to be on the safe side, she and Robin decided to change the direction of Sarah's lutz approach for the Olympics.

Sarah felt much more confident about her lutz. "It's much better, and I'd like people to compare [my lutz] with other people's now," she told *Time*.

Then, as the icing on the cake, Sarah and Robin decided to add another triple jump to Sarah's long program. Adding another triple was risky. Every time a skater goes into a jump, she chances a fall. But if the jump is successful, her scores go up.

Sarah originally had two triples in her program. But she pulled one of them out because the reward didn't seem worth the risk.

Now it was time to put it back in. "I was coming to the Olympics as the third-place finisher

[Above] Sarah, age 12, executes a spiral in practice.

[Below] Sarah and coach Robin Wagner react as Sarah's scores are announced at the 2002 U.S. Figure Skating Championships, putting Sarah in third place.

[This page, above] Sarah skates her way to second place overall at the 2001 U.S. Skating Championship in Boston.

[This page, below] Sarah salutes the crowd after nabbing first place in the Mastercard Skate Canada International Ladies' competition.

[Next page, left] Exuberant from the previous night's gold medal performance, Sarah treats fans to another beautiful skate at the Olympic figure skating exhibition on Friday, February 22nd.

[Next page, above right] Skating her heart out in the Olympic women's short program.

[Next page, below right] Embraced by her two biggest fans—parents John and Amy Hughes—after winning gold.

[This page, above] Smiling as always—Sarah performs in the Olympic free skate program.

[This page, below] Bursting with happiness, Sarah leans down as the Olympic gold medal is placed around her neck.

[Next page] Sarah arches back gracefully during her Olympic free skate program.

[Previous page, above] Back to school! Sarah walks in front of Great Neck North High School on her first day back after winning Olympic gold.

[Previous page, below] A hometown hero, in more ways than one! Garry Siele, co-owner of Deli on the Green in Sarah's Great Neck, NY, hometown, displays the sandwich now named after Sarah.

[This page] Turning the tables—Sarah gets a chance to present an award when she joins members of the Backstreet Boys to present the 2002 Grammy for best pop collaboration with vocals. The winner? "Lady Maramalade" from the *Moulin Rouge* soundtrack (Christina Aguilera, Lil Kim, Mya and Pink).

[Left] A glowing Sarah proudly supports her team, the NY Rangers, giving fans a quick wave before dropping the ceremonial first puck in a game against the Philadelphia Flyers at Madison Square Garden.

[Above right] The ultimate homecoming: Sarah and coach Robin Wagner share the crowd's excitement as they ride together down the road temporarily renamed "Sarah Hughes Way" for the parade in her honor on March 10, 2002.

[Below right] Sarah shows off her new key to the city, presented by New York mayor Mike Bloomberg.

from our country, so I needed to pull out everything I could," she would later explain to *Sports Illustrated*.

Making the U.S. Olympic team had already given Sarah more publicity than she'd ever had before. The local Long Island papers were full of stories about her Olympic debut. Then the Olympics brought her something else: her first major national coverage.

The Olympic Preview issue of *Time* magazine would feature Sarah on its cover!

Time was taking a chance on this one. *Newsweek* had chosen Michelle Kwan. *Sports Illustrated* highlighted Russian superstar Irina Slutskaya.

But the Olympics is all about young athletes doing the unexpected. Athletes like Sarah, who have toiled in the obscurity of their sport until the Olympics propels them into the headlines.

If the Olympics could make Peggy Fleming and Tara Lipinski famous, why not Sarah Hughes?

The February 11, 2002, issue of *Time* shows Sarah leaping into the air above Salt Lake City's Wasatch peaks. In her sparkly pink Tania Bass dress, she looks light and joyous and ready to take on the world. The article enthusiastically rates her chances for an Olympic medal. Under the heading "Why Hughes is a Good Skate," reporter Alice Park writes:

"Hughes has already beaten Kwan and Slutskaya, the top contenders for the gold, and has a good chance of doing so again, as long as she keeps her nerves in check. The technical difficulty of her jump combinations sets her apart from Kwan, while her growing lyricism easily exceeds that of Slutskaya. Self-described as 'stupid competitive,' Hughes has more international experience than teammate Cohen and feels a strong sense of duty to represent her country well in her first Olympics."

As if Sarah weren't under enough pressure already!

Finally, it was almost time for Sarah to leave for Salt Lake City. She had covered every base she could think of. One more time, she went over her mental list:

New music. *Check.*

New hairdo. *Check.*

New dresses. *Check.*

New triple jump. *Check.*

Much-improved lutz. *Check.*

Oh, and there was one more thing. Sarah couldn't forget her special Peggy Fleming

T-shirt—the one her old friend Peggy had sent her with the note, "PF's PJs." Sarah always slept in a Peggy Fleming T-shirt before a meet. She believed it brought her good luck.

She was going to need it!

CHAPTER FIVE:

Let the Games Begin

Click!

Sarah gave a big smile. She was having her picture taken with President George W. Bush and First Lady Laura Bush. It was February 8, 2002, and she was at the opening ceremony of the Olympics. Along with her other teammates, Sarah had marched into the Olympic arena behind a big American flag.

Sarah planned to stay two nights in the Olympic Village with the other athletes and try to soak up the atmosphere. Already she'd met some of her fellow teammates. She was thrilled when some of them, like ski champion Jonny Moseley, recognized her. But she wasn't surprised when they didn't. It only gave Sarah more incentive to make sure her

Olympic performance was strong enough to earn her the widespread recognition she still didn't quite have. Snowboarder Danny Kass tried to convince her *he* was a figure skater. Only later did she let him know she was the real thing.

But Sarah couldn't have too much fun—yet. She was here to work. The first ladies' figure skating event, the short program, wouldn't be held until February 19, a whole week and a half away. In the meantime, Sarah had to practice that troublesome lutz. And she needed to do it in a low pressure environment—exactly what Salt Lake City *wasn't* during all the frenzy and excitement of the Olympics.

She and Robin hopped on a plane to Colorado Springs, where she could train at the World Arena for six days. There they could find quiet and privacy, away from the noisy chaos of the Games. Other women skaters left, too—Sasha Cohen went home to Lake Arrowhead, California. Irina Slutskaya was still in Russia. Only Michelle Kwan remained in Salt Lake to work out at a separate rink.

The week was quiet and uneventful. Sarah

trained, had her nails done, signed a few autographs, got a massage. Every day she talked to her parents back home on Long Island and e-mailed a few friends. At night she and Robin would stay up and watch the Olympics. They got hooked, just like the rest of the country.

The only break in the routine was when designer Jef Billings and his seamstress flew in from Los Angeles with the brand-new costumes. This would be Sarah's first fitting, even though the event was only a week away. In Los Angeles, Billings had made a special Sarah Hughes mannequin based on the measurements she had sent him. Now Sarah got to model the outfits for the first time.

They were *gorgeous*. Just what Sarah and Robin had been looking for. Sarah wanted them to be a surprise. She made Robin promise she wouldn't tell anyone what they looked like until she wore them for competition. She wanted to make a dramatic debut.

On Friday afternoon, February 15, Sarah flew back to Salt Lake City. Even now she stayed away from the Olympic Village, settling in with Robin at a hotel a short distance away.

Early the next morning Sarah stepped onto the ice at the Delta Center in Salt Lake City. The last time she'd been there was for the 1999 Nationals. She'd been only thirteen then, awed by the other skaters and a bit unsure of herself. Now she was sixteen, self-assured, and a contender for an Olympic medal.

So much had changed in three short years.

But she loved being back. "It's a warm rink, it has a warm feeling," Sarah told *Newsday*. "And there are Olympic rings everywhere you look. I was so eager to get in the rink."

This time, she had a few good practices on that rink. Skating well in the practices is important because the judges attend and take notes. They watch to see what moves the skaters are having difficulty on, and which ones they perform easily. That way, when they watch the actual competition later on, they'll already have an estimate of what the skater will get. Depending on the performance, the final marks they award can go way up—or way down.

No wonder Sarah got new outfits just for the practices!

It wasn't just the judges who were watching the skaters. Skaters were watching each other, too. On the rink with Sarah during those practices were the best ladies' ice skaters in the world.

Michelle Kwan. Irina Slutskaya. Sasha Cohen. And twenty-three others.

Sarah had competed against twenty-one-year-old Michelle Kwan more times than against any of the other skaters. That was because Michelle is an American. It was also because she had been the national champion for the past six years, as long as Sarah had been skating in Senior events. She was the four-time world champion, too.

At thirteen, Michelle became the youngest U.S. Olympic Festival champion ever. By the time she was fifteen, she was both U.S. and world champion. But she lost the gold in both to Tara Lipinski in 1997.

For a while, it didn't look as if she'd have the chance to regain it. For two months before the 1998 Nationals, Michelle was off the ice with an injury. Rumors flew that she wouldn't even be able to skate. But she proved them wrong. What happened next has become ice-skating legend.

Skating to the music of Rachmaninoff,

Michelle wowed the crowd with the most perfect short program anyone had ever seen. Her free skate was just as breathtaking. She received seven perfect 6.0s on her short program and eight 6.0s on the free skate! It was a new national record—and has never been broken since.

Michelle's first Olympics were at Lillehammer, Norway in 1994, as an alternate. Michelle worked out by herself on a rink far from the center of the action. "It didn't feel like an Olympic experience," Michelle said later. "I never got to see the ice rink. I never really got to see the Olympic village."

After that, she vowed to go to the Nagano games in 1998 as a regular contestant. She did, and she skated superbly. If it had been any other Olympics, she would have won. But she lost by a hair to a tiny fifteen-year-old ball of energy named Tara Lipinski. Michelle had to be satisfied with the silver.

So Michelle had come to the 2002 Olympics with something to prove. But some observers said that her performances weren't as strong as they could be. She was having trouble with jumps. She had been trying for years to learn a triple salchow-triple loop combination. Sarah could do one. So could Michelle's main Russian rival, Irina Slutskaya.

But not Michelle. She was known for her artistic excellence, not her athleticism.

There was no doubt that Michelle Kwan was one of the greatest women skaters of all time. But would she prove it at these Olympics?

Many people thought that Michelle's most serious competition was Russian fireball Irina Slutskaya. Animated and athletic, Irina was known for her spectacular jumps and explosive energy. With her brilliant smile and apple-red cheeks, she could light up an arena.

Irina had finished in second place to Michelle three times at the World Championships. But she beat Michelle in other international competitions six times in two years. As far as she was concerned, the Olympic gold medal was up for grabs.

Irina's spins and jumps were certainly superior to Michelle's, everyone agreed. But Michelle kept earning higher marks for presentation.

What would happen at the Olympics was anyone's guess. Irina herself told *Sports*

Illustrated, "Both Sarah and Michelle will do well. I'm sure of it. They're strong. I need to fight for my place."

And fight she would.

Then there was the hot new star, Sasha Cohen. Sarah had first encountered Sasha at the 2000 U.S. Championships. That year the fifteen-year-old Sasha skated a nearly flawless program to win silver to Sarah's bronze. The next year Sasha was out with a back injury. But when she came back, she came back strong, beating Sarah once again at the 2002 Nationals. Now Sasha, not Sarah, was the new kid on the block.

Sarah didn't like it one bit.

Only 5'1", Sasha had the petite energy of Tara Lipinski. Her Charlotte spirals were breathtaking. Her jumps were light and quick, her spins fluid and flexible.

Audiences loved her.

Judges did, too.

Sasha at her best was very good indeed. She was just starting her international career. And she was clearly aiming for the very top.

But then, so was Sarah. And Michelle, Irina, and twenty-three other skaters.

Only one of them would make it.

As Sarah finished her practice the morning of February 19, she gave the arena one last look.

The next time she saw it, she would be skating in the short program at the Winter Olympics!

CHAPTER
SIX:

Short and Sweet

"I'm number five!" Sarah told Robin Wagner at midday on Monday. Sarah meant that she would skate fifth in the ladies' short program on Tuesday night. Robin shook her head. This wasn't good news.

The day had started briskly, with a forty-five-minute practice session at the Delta Arena. Then came the event of the day—the drawing that would determine where in the lineup the twenty-seven skaters would go the following evening.

All the skaters filed into a room for the drawing. In the front, the referee had a little velvet bag full of poker chips. On each chip was a number representing one of the nineteen countries represented in the event. The Armenian skater drew first and pulled out number 10, representing Japan. Then the 10 was put back into the bag, and the Japanese skaters came up to pick their numbers. Everyone else followed alphabetically by country.

Sarah put her hand into the bag and drew out a chip. She looked at it and handed it to the referee. An assistant entered the number into the computer. A moment later, the number appeared on the big screen in the front of the room:

Sarah Hughes: number 5.

Sasha Cohen got number 6. Irina Slutskaya would be number 13, and Michelle Kwan number 15. That meant that of all the likely medal candidates, Sarah would go first.

This could be a problem, as Sarah well knew. Judges tend to score low in the beginning of an event. They want to leave lots of room for skaters to receive high scores later on.

Sarah would have to do so well the others would have difficulty catching up!

She'd get two sets of marks from the judges: one for required elements and one for presentation. There were eight required elements in the evening's short program:

1) a double axel;
2) a double or triple jump;

3) a jump combination (double and triple or two triples);
4) a flying spin;
5) a layback spin;
6) a spin combination;
7) a spiral-step sequence; and
8) a step sequence.

For her combination jump, Sarah had chosen a triple lutz-double toe loop.

Judges were required to deduct points for mistakes made on the required elements: -0.5 for falling on a jump or spin; -0.4 for turning a triple into a double or a double into a single; -0.3 for landing on two feet; -0.1 to 0.2 for touching a hand to the ice.

And −0.3 for a flutz!

For the presentation marks, judges would be evaluating artistic merit. This was a more personal judgment, but still based on particular criteria. They looked at the beauty of the choreography. The skater's timing and ease of movement. The way she expressed the mood of the music. Her carriage and style. Her originality. The complexity of the footwork.

Presentation takes into account all the intangibles that make up a great performance.

Judges reward a skater's enthusiasm and love for what she is doing. That's why figure skating is not just athletic performance. It's dramatic presentation and ballet, too.

All scores, for the short and long programs, are based on a 6.0 scale: 0 means the skater didn't skate at all; 1 means she skated very badly; 2 means she skated poorly; 3 means she was mediocre; 4 means she skated well; 5 means she skated very well; and 6 means she skated perfectly.

Then each set of scores is added up into a total score. At the end of the short program, Sarah would have nine total scores, one from each judge. Let's say, for instance, that the judge from Canada gave her a 5.2 for required elements and a 5.5 for presentation, for a total of 10.7. She'd have eight other totals, too. Her scores would then be fed into a computer. It would assign her a standing—1,2,3, etc.—by comparing her totals to those of the other skaters.

In short, Sarah's final standing would depend not on the marks she got but on the marks she got compared to those of other skaters.

She would just have to do her best and see what happened!

*   *   *

The crowd roared.

Sarah Hughes stepped out onto the ice for the short program at the 2002 Olympics and the stands went wild.

Wow, she thought. She wasn't used to so much enthusiasm. This was a mostly American audience, and the hometown crowd was especially patriotic this year. But she hadn't expected so much noise!

If Sarah had looked up, she would have seen the whole Hughes family in the stands. Rebecca, David, Matt, Emily, and Taylor were waving a fifteen-foot white-and-blue banner. It read: HUGHES GOTTA BELIEVE. Her parents, John and Amy, were in another part of the arena.

Sarah clasped her hands together in silent prayer.

Then she skated around the side of the arena to give herself time to focus. She shook her legs, took a deep breath, and skated to center ice.

She was ready.

The crowd fell quiet. The soaring chords of "Ave Maria" floated into the rink, and Sarah set up her first jump. As she skated forward, the long navy blue sleeves of her new Jef Billings dress fluttered in the breeze. The dress Billings had promised would be ecclesiastical was indeed elegant, with classic, flowing lines. A rhinestone pattern swooped above her waist like a church steeple.

She was up in the air for her first double axel—

And she nailed it! The jump felt wonderful.

Now if she could just get through that tricky combination jump . . .

Backward she sped, heading toward the corner of the rink. She took off on the edge of her skate for the triple lutz.

And sure enough, it was the wrong edge. Off in the sidelines, Robin shook her head. After all her months of work, Sarah had flutzed the jump after all!

But that wasn't the only problem. Sarah had skated far too close to the board. When she landed her double loop, she had to scrunch herself up and pull her leg behind her to avoid hitting the side of the rink.

Whew! She didn't touch anything.

Halfway through the program, her jumps were over. Sarah was so relieved she clapped and pumped her hands. She sailed through the rest of her program with a big grin on her face.

Her program wasn't perfect, she knew. But it

was awfully good. Best of all, there were no major flaws.

Over on the "kiss and cry" bench a minute later, she gave Robin a big hug. Then they settled back to wait for the judges' marks.

The technical marks flitted across the screen first. It was worse than she'd thought, in the low to mid-fives. There was even a 5.1 and a 5.2 from the Russian and German judges.

Ouch!

Robin gave her hand a squeeze. The presentation marks were bound to be better.

And they were, in the 5.6 range overall.

Sarah was in first place after her program, but she knew that meant little. Twenty-two skaters had yet to skate!

Sarah waved to the crowds for the last time that night, and she and Robin went back to the locker rooms to wait. They wouldn't be watching the rest of the contest, but they could hear the crowd.

It roared again. This time it was for Sasha Cohen, next on the ice after Sarah.

Sasha sped out onto the rink, determined and self-assured.

For Sasha, this was also her first Olympic experience. "Once they called my name, no butterflies, just calm," Sasha told reporters afterward.

She gave one of her best performances ever. Her long spiral was exquisite. Her jumps soared. And her spin was spun gold.

The crowd went wild. Here was the great new skater they had been waiting for. This time, she was even better than Sarah Hughes.

Judges thought so, too. Sasha's technical scores were 5.6 to 5.8 and her presentation marks 5.8.

"I just thought to myself, 'You have one chance,'" Sasha commented. "I didn't want any regrets. I wanted to fight for everything."

Sarah immediately dropped down to second in the standings. But she had expected that. The question was would she drop still further?

The two favorites were still to come.

Irina Slutskaya was also in top form that night. Her triple-double combinations were breathtakingly high. Six of the nine judges placed her above Sasha.

And Sarah Hughes slipped still further in the ranking, to third.

Michelle Kwan was next.

The standing ovation that Michelle received

when she stepped into the rink startled even the veteran.

She hadn't even skated yet!

But the American audience was excited to see Michelle and excited to see her do well. She didn't disappoint. Although Michelle's technical difficulty was not as advanced as Sarah's or Sasha's or Irina's, her artistic brilliance was on display for all to behold.

Yes, her triple flip had only two, not three, rotations. But her long, joyous spiral more than made up for it.

When she finished, Michelle punched the air in triumph. She'd done it!

In the kiss and cry area, she hugged her father and sat down to wait for the results. Not surprisingly, her technical marks weren't great. They ranged from 5.5 to 5.9. On the bench, Michelle reacted with a thumbs down.

"Come on, come on!" she said impatiently.

Finally the marks for presentation rolled across the screen.

A row of nearly perfect 5.9s!

Michelle Kwan was officially in first place in the 2002 Olympics after the short program. Irina Slutskaya was in second. Sasha Cohen was in third.

And Sarah Hughes was in fourth.

Sarah was high enough in the standings to still get a medal. And low enough to slip off the podium altogether.

It all depended on how she did in the long program on Thursday night.

Sarah didn't know what the next two days would bring. She knew only one thing.

Everything depended on her next skate!

Chapter
Seven:

A Dream Come True

Sarah Hughes had had high hopes for a medal coming into the Olympics. But now, with her fourth-place finish after the short program, it looked as if her chances were slipping away.

Was Sarah angry? Was she upset?

No, she was happy!

"I think it hurt me to skate so early," Sarah said to the press the next morning. "But overall, I'm happy. I almost hit the boards, but I didn't touch them and I came out clean."

If she had to score herself, she added with a smile, she'd go for a 5.8 or a 5.9!

Her family was just as upbeat about her performance.

"She skated great," her sister Rebecca told *Newsday*. "Your heart races when she skates.

You're so nervous. And to see her land all her jumps in an arena like this with all that pressure is incredible."

John Hughes agreed. "I saw her just before she skated," the proud father said. "And she looked the best I've ever seen her, confident and gorgeous. And the audience was terrific."

Obviously her family knew something everyone else didn't know: Sarah was ready to fight.

She'd always done well as the underdog, coming in from behind. As her coach put it, "Sarah's better as a chaser, not as the one being chased. It fires up something inside of her."

Now Sarah was motivated as never before. The important thing was to stay focused. Sarah spent the two days before her big night in her usual routine: a morning practice, lunch, exercise, answering the hundreds of good-luck e-mails she received from friends around the world. She was quiet, focused, trying to concentrate.

NBC commentators who were watching the final practice on Thursday morning agreed that Sarah had the best showing there.

"The fourth-place finish might have ignited a little competitive fire," former gold medalist

Scott Hamilton said as he watched rinkside.

That afternoon after a nap, Sarah killed time by watching *The Simpsons*. It wasn't one of her favorite shows, but her brothers loved it. Now she'd have a few more jokes to trade with them.

Usually she, Robin, and Robin's husband, Jerry, talked about current events—politics, or that day's *New York Times*—in the last suspenseful hours before a major event. About anything but the all-important skate coming up.

This time, Sarah deliberately turned the conversation to the long program. What, she asked Jerry, would it take for her to win a gold medal?

"You would have to skate brilliantly," Jerry told her, "and Irina would have to beat Michelle—but not you."

Without missing a beat, Sarah said, "Okay. I'll do it!"

She wasn't due to warm up until eight-forty that night. But Robin made sure they arrived at the Delta Center early, by seven-thirty. Sarah was known for her casual attitude toward time. Her coach wanted to make sure that on this night of all nights, they weren't late.

Just before the warm-ups started, Sarah

slipped into her new lavender Billings outfit. It had 10,000 beads, and it sparkled when she moved. It was definitely a wow!

Once again, Sarah would skate first among the four medal contenders. She held Robin's hand for a moment before she skated onto the ice. "I know. I'll let the music start first," she assured her coach.

Then Sarah took a deep breath. This was it. This was her big chance. All her life she'd dreamed of being in the free skate at the Olympics, and now she was here.

She would hold nothing back.

She'd show everyone what she could do.

Twenty seconds into the four-minute program, Sarah landed a double axel. The audience of 16,500 roared its approval, and Sarah grinned in growing confidence.

Just three minutes and forty seconds to go. Her most difficult jump was coming up—a triple salchow-triple loop.

Off at the sideboards, Robin tensed her body as Sarah prepared for the move. Robin leaped up into the air—

As out on the ice, Sarah soared in two gravity-defying rotations. She made a clean landing. The crowd bellowed with pleasure.

Yes! Sarah thought, her face lighting up in a broad smile.

Now for that pesky triple lutz. . . .

She set up and took off—on the correct edge this time.

Good-bye, flutz. Hello, lutz. The spell was broken!

Robin pumped her fists in triumph.

Another setup and another triple. Done and done. Sarah was nailing them all, letting go and allowing her body to do what it had been training to do for the past thirteen years. All those five o'clock in the morning wake-ups, all those ballet lessons and workouts and pep talks, all those hours in the car and hours on the ice . . . this was what they had come to. A perfect skate. The skate of a lifetime.

It was halfway into the program, and the momentum was growing. Something magical was happening, and everyone in the arena could feel it. This was why they loved skating. This was why they had come to the Olympics. To see the beauty. To feel the excitement. To see a young skater skating her heart out and loving every minute of it.

Skating history was being made before their eyes.

If only Sarah could keep it up. Please, everyone prayed. Don't let her make a mistake!

Sarah skated on in growing exhilaration. Her second triple-triple combination was coming up, the one she and Robin had added in those action-packed three weeks before the Olympics. This was the move that was supposed to give her the edge she needed. To put her way out ahead of the pack.

In a dizzying burst of speed, Sarah flew up in her first spin. Around and around and around she flew. Her foot touched the ice, the edge of her skate pushed off, and up she flew again. Around and around and around.

In the coaching area, Robin was jumping up and down, too. She could hardly believe what was happening.

Easily, gracefully, Sarah landed her jump.

I did it! she exulted. Even though the program wasn't over yet, she couldn't help herself. She clapped her hands and shrieked.

It had happened. For the first time ever anywhere, a woman had landed two triple-triple jumps in competition. This wasn't just a personal best—it was a world record!

The audience let out its breath and roared. Now they knew that Sarah Hughes wasn't going to let them down. Just like Sarah, they were caught up in a wave of excitement.

The last ninety seconds flew by in a joyous rush. The music quickened, and Sarah let herself go. As the crescendo built, she swirled through spirals, spins, another triple, breathtaking leaps, at dizzying speed. The crowd, completely carried away, grew louder and louder.

Finally with her final spin combination, the whole house rose to its feet in a standing ovation. It was so loud that Sarah couldn't hear the music anymore.

She spun to a halt, even before the final chords of music sounded.

Dozens of stuffed animals and bouquets began to rain down upon the ice.

Sarah was ecstatic. Beaming, she raised her arms in triumph. "Wow," was all she could say to herself. "Wow." With both hands, she threw kisses back to the crowd.

Never in her wildest dreams had she imagined such a skate. Never had she imagined such an audience.

Never had she imagined such a night.

She turned to face Robin on the sidelines and raised her shoulders in a giant shrug. Can you believe it? her wide eyes seemed to say.

Robin opened her arms in welcome. "I love you!" she shrieked.

Sarah rushed to hug her coach. But Robin wouldn't let her leave the ice yet.

"Turn around," she told the girl she'd spent four long, hard-working years with. "Close your eyes, soak it in."

And Sarah did. The crowd kept cheering. Wow!

When Sarah finally left the ice, tears of joy were streaming down her face. But it wasn't over yet. She still had to hear from the judges, who were busy tallying their scores.

She and Robin retreated to the kiss and cry bench to wait it out. Robin put her arm around her, and Sarah waved to her family and friends at home. They knew the audience loved her. But how would the judges react?

The answer came a few minutes later as the marks for technical merit flashed on the screen:

5.7 5.8 5.8 5.8 5.8 5.8 5.7 5.8 5.8

Sarah gasped in delight. The marks were wonderful! They were the best she could have wished for.

Then the marks for presentation went up.

5.7 5.7 5.8 5.6 5.8 5.8 5.8 5.8 5.8

These scores were great, too. Of course, they weren't perfect. By not giving her any 5.9s or 6.0s, the judges had obviously left plenty of room for other skaters to get high marks later. But still, it appeared that Sarah might have done well enough to win a medal.

Strangely enough, medals were not on Sarah's mind as she left the rink a moment later. She was still elated by her own performance, and she couldn't stop beaming. As she said to an NBC interviewer rinkside, "I just wanted to have fun. Tonight I just said I have nothing to lose. I never skated that well in my whole life."

Robin and Sarah left for an empty men's locker room where they would remain while the other top skaters finished their programs. An NBC cameraman asked if he could film them as they reacted to the evening's events.

Okay, they agreed. Robin wasn't sure, though, that this was the right thing to do. She joked to *Newsday* later that she'd worried that if she and Sarah looked too happy, people might think they were obnoxious. If they looked too sad, people might think they were sore losers!

But it was too late. The deed was done. When Robin and Sarah settled down on a bench to wait for the results, the camera was on them. Soon Sarah would find out whether she had won a medal at the Olympics. And millions of people around the world would be watching.

Next up: Sasha Cohen, skating to the dramatic music of Bizet's opera *Carmen*. In true Spanish style, Sasha was wearing a flame-colored dress and a red rosette in her hair. She struck a striking opening pose and the audience sighed in anticipation.

This should be great.

Sasha started off brilliantly. A great performer, she leaped and twirled and spun with an energy worthy of Bizet's fiery heroine.

Then it happened. She went up on her only triple jump of the evening—a triple lutz-triple toe combination—and fell on the landing.

Sasha put her hand on the ice to catch herself and grimaced slightly. Had she thrown away her chance for a medal?

Gamely she picked herself up and went on

with her program. Now the audience was tense, worried that she might fall again.

She did not. But Sasha had been rattled by the fall. Her landings were not as clean as they could have been. The entrance to her spin was cut short.

Despite her elegant sense of style, Sasha did not have the skate she had hoped for.

Her marks reflected her difficulties. She received one 5.5 and three 5.6s on technical merit, and even one 5.5 on presentation. The remaining 5.7s and 5.8s were not enough to lift her above Sarah.

In the locker room, Robin nervously called her husband, who was sitting in the stands. How had Sasha done? she asked him.

Not to worry, he replied. She hadn't done well enough.

Sarah was guaranteed at least a bronze medal at the 2002 Olympics!

Robin took the opportunity to remind Sarah about winning etiquette. No matter what color medal she ended up with, Sarah should be gracious and smiling. She'd had a miraculous skate that had earned her millions of new fans. She should be thankful!

As it turned out, the little talk wasn't needed.

*   *   *

The two front-runners were still to come: Michelle Kwan and Irina Slutskaya.

Michelle was up first, skating in an elegant scarlet dress with gold trim. She would be performing to the music of Rimsky-Korsakov's *Scheherazade*. As she came out, the audience gave her an enthusiastic ovation.

Gifted and dedicated, Michelle had been in the public eye for a very long time. She was a national champion and a world champion many times over. The only honor that had eluded her was that Olympic gold medal.

Everyone knew that Michelle lacked the athleticism of Irina or Sarah. But if she could just jump cleanly, she'd be fine. She'd been first coming out of the short program, after all. For sheer loveliness on ice, no one could beat her.

But it was not to be. As soon as Michelle started her skate, it was clear she would not create magic that night.

From the first, Michelle seemed to lack confidence. Her only planned triple-triple combination of the evening morphed into a triple-double instead, and she landed the jump on both feet instead of one.

Then, halfway through her program, Michelle fell out of a triple flip and put her hand to the ice to steady herself.

The audience groaned.

She recovered and went on. But the evening was over for Michelle. Disappointment was etched in every line of her body. As the audience cheered her on, Michelle finished her program. She even turned another double jump into a triple.

But by the time she ended, Michelle could barely manage to smile and wave to her fans. She was in shock.

Maybe the judges would go easy on her. Maybe they'd focus on her artistry and ignore her technical mistakes. She still had hope as she climbed into the kiss and cry area to be with her father, who looked grave.

Michelle got five mediocre 5.6s for technical merit, relieved only by a few 5.7s and one 5.8. In presentation she fared better, racking up 5.9s and a slew of 5.8s.

Michelle Kwan had definitely lost the gold. The best she could hope for was silver. Whether she got it depended on Irina Slutskaya.

Irina knew the gold could be hers if she just reached out and grabbed it. Because she had come in second in the short program, she had an advantage over Sarah. But the twenty-three-year-old Russian was under enormous pressure. Would she be able to pull off a great performance?

She would be skating to Verdi's *Tosca*. But it was clear from the start that Irina's program wasn't her best. She seemed tentative, slow. A planned triple turned into a double, and she came dangerously close to a fall during a triple flip, catching herself just in time.

Irina was a pro. But she was definitely having an off night. How would the judges react?

In the locker room, Sarah and Robin held their breath.

Out in the rink, the suspense mounted. The scoring was complicated, and the judges checked and double-checked. Even the NBC commentators weren't sure what was going on.

"If it's a three-way tie, Sarah gets the gold," Hamilton told the television audience. But was it a tie?

"Okayyy—this is no pressure point," Sarah joked to relieve the tension.

One minute passed, then two, then three. Finally, the judges announced Irina's marks to the waiting world: mostly 5.8s and one 5.9 on technical merit. A range of marks from 5.6 to 5.9 on presentation.

What did it all mean?

In the locker room the NBC cameraman listened in on his headphones. Then he leaned forward to speak to Sarah.

"You've won the gold!"

Golden Girl

Gold? An Olympic gold?

"Oh my God," Sarah shrieked. "Oh my God, this is unbelievable." She clutched Robin and tumbled off the bench to the floor.

"The gold medal of the Olympics!" Robin screamed. The two hugged and cried while the cameraman caught it all on videotape.

"I didn't think it was possible," Sarah exclaimed.

But it was. As Robin's husband had told her, Sarah would win if she beat Irina in the long program and Irina beat Michelle. That was just what had happened. But the results were even more complicated. When the marks for the long and short programs were added up, Irina and Sarah were tied for first place. When that happens, the gold goes to the person who comes in first in the long program.

That person was Sarah Hughes.

Nobody coming into the arena that evening had expected such an astounding outcome.

Even commentator Scott Hamilton seemed in shock. "What an upset!" he shouted on TV.

Sarah's parents were as awed as everyone else. Although they had seats in the audience, Amy Hughes left the rink before her daughter started to skate. Watching her was just too nerve-racking. So Amy went out and started wandering the concourse.

As soon as Sarah left the kiss and cry area, the first thing she did was call her mom. "She never does that," Amy told reporters the next day. "She wanted to know what I thought. She was so happy. When it's your kid, that's all you want. I didn't care what the other skaters did. I didn't even watch."

John Hughes left the arena next, to find his wife and tell her the good news. After he called her, he saw his son Matt standing in front of a monitor. Matt, who had been sitting next to his brothers and sisters in the arena, had also left after Sarah's program. He had a psychology class at Ithaca College the next day, and he wanted to catch a flight out.

Together they watched the show on the concourse TV. Sasha Cohen fell. Michelle stumbled. And Irina slipped.

"I'm thinking, 'Wait a minute. Something is going to happen,'" Matt told *Newsday* the next day.

Sure enough, a few minutes later the words "Sarah Hughes, gold" flashed on the screen.

What? What happened? John and Matt shouted.

Just then a jubilant Amy ran up to them. "How is that possible?" she asked.

That's just what reporters were asking Sarah.

How had she pulled off the most stunning upset of the Olympics?

Sarah was still bubbling. "Going in I didn't think I had a chance for gold, let alone a medal, given who was skating here," she said with a broad smile. "So I didn't hold back."

She giggled. "It's wonderful. I didn't know what the judges were thinking. I can't wait to go to the podium."

Sarah Hughes had just become the seventh American woman to win the gold medal in ladies' figure skating. She did it by pulling off the most technically advanced skate ever. She was the first woman to successfully complete two triple-triple combinations in an Olympic competition. And she was the first woman to win after earning fourth place in the short program. This had never happened in the Olympics before.

In short, Sarah had made history!

The group of women champions that Sarah had joined was very small and select. By becoming the "seventh sister," she had joined some of the most accomplished and famous women in U.S. sports:

• There was Tenley Albright, winner of the 1956 gold medal at Cortina d'Ampezzo, Italy. Tenley had actually turned to skating as therapy for childhood polio. She followed up her triumphs on the ice by graduating from Harvard Medical School and becoming a surgeon.

• Carol Heiss won at Squaw Valley, California, in 1960. The five-time world champion quit skating for a show-business career but made only one movie, *Snow White and the Three Stooges*. After raising her three children, she returned to figure skating eighteen years later as a coach.

• The magical Peggy Fleming won the hearts of Americans with her unprecedented performance at Grenoble, France, in 1968. After winning the World Championships later that year, she joined the touring show Ice Follies and began a professional career on ice. The first skating TV star, Peggy Fleming inspired a whole generation of young girls to become skaters. She has been working as a TV commentator since 1981.

• Dorothy Hamill wowed everyone with her charm and skill at the 1976 Olympics in Innsbruck, Austria. Within a month, her trademark wedge haircut had been adopted by thousands of girls across the country. After winning the World Championships later that year, she quit competition and joined the Ice Capades. She has been a professional ice skater ever since.

• Kristi Yamaguchi won a surprise gold at Albertville, France, in 1992. It was a surprise because up until two years earlier, Kristi had been a doubles as well as singles skater. It is almost unheard of to do well in both. After her win, she took to the professional circuit full time. Today she is one of the regulars in Stars on Ice.

• Fifteen-year-old Tara Lipinski, the youngest person ever to earn an individual Olympic gold medal in skating, won hers at Nagano, Japan in 1998. Today Tara continues to skate for Stars on Ice.

Sarah knew these women coming into the Olympics, but she would get to know them even better after joining their ranks.

"I thought she was just spectacular," Peggy Fleming told *The New York Times* the day after the competition. "She moved across the ice with such flow and speed and joy. I've never seen her skate that well before."

And at a party Friday morning, Dorothy Hamill asked Sarah to sign her copy of *Time* magazine with Sarah's picture on the cover. Sarah wrote to her longtime idol, "Dorothy, thank you for all the inspiration. Love, Sarah."

While Sarah was celebrating, the other contestants were adjusting to the news.

Irina Slutskaya was disappointed at first, of

course. But she had earned a silver, after all—her first Olympic medal. By the time of the medal presentations, Irina was smiling.

Seventeen-year-old Sasha Cohen, who left without a medal, was disappointed, too. But she knew she was lucky just to have been there. Sasha still had her best skating years ahead of her.

Michelle Kwan, though, faced a bigger challenge. She had worked so hard for so long, yet the gold medal had slipped from her grasp. Still, when she came out for the medal presentation, the crowd, eager to show their love, gave her a big ovation.

Then it was Sarah's turn. She came into the rink last, her face glowing.

When she was eight, she had predicted, "When I grow up I'm going to win the gold medal at the Olympics."

Now she had.

She turned to climb onto the first-place podium but didn't know how to get up there. With her hand, Michelle motioned her over to the third-place platform. Step up here, she was saying.

One by one, each winner bowed her head to receive her medal. Bronze for Michelle. Silver for Irina. Gold for Sarah.

And a bouquet of bright yellow daffodils for each of them.

"Ladies and gentlemen," the announcer boomed. "Will you please rise for the national anthem of the United States of America."

Head raised proudly, Sarah sang the familiar words: "Oh say can you see, by the dawn's early light . . ."

She cried. Her Olympic moment had arrived.

CHAPTER
NINE:

Anything Is Possible

"Of course it was a miracle," Sarah said on the *Today Show* the next morning. Her eyes twinkled. "What are the chances of this happening?"

It was 6:45 A.M. central time on Friday. Sarah Hughes was running on two hours of sleep and adrenaline. After the medals ceremony the night before, she met her whole family for a late-night dinner. It was a joyous reunion.

"Everybody wanted to see my medal," Sarah told Katie Couric. "I haven't seen them in so long, and they all were saying, 'Where's the medal? Where's the medal?' I said, 'Hey, guys, what about me?'"

Amy Hughes had been amazed that her children were all there together—and up so late! It was already one o'clock in the morning. But winning a gold medal was a once-in-a-lifetime occasion.

Meanwhile, John Hughes and Robin Wagner were answering hundreds of e-mail messages from all over the country. The *Today Show* wanted Sarah the next morning. The Grammys wanted her later that week. Leno called. Rosie O'Donnell. *Saturday Night Live*.

Sarah was suddenly the hottest new celebrity in the country.

But to John Hughes, his daughter was still a teenager who needed her sleep. She had an exhibition show to skate at the Olympics the next evening. And it looked as if the week was shaping up to be a big one.

It was definitely time for the long, extraordinary night to end. Sarah took her medal off to bed with her—and slept with it. A few hours later, she was in a car and zooming up the road for the *Today Show* interview. Sarah had overslept.

The hoopla was just beginning. Overnight, the national press had picked up the story, and now everyone wanted to interview Sarah. "Sarah's Gold Rush!" the New York *Daily News* blared. "By Leaps and Bounds!" a *Sports*

Illustrated cover exulted. "Gold!" *Newsday* said simply.

At a press conference after her 8 A.M. practice, Sarah was happy to keep talking about her skate. "I always go out and I'm always so worried about whether I'm going to do this jump or that or skate fast or spin well," she said. "Last night I just went out and I just skated. I didn't realize it until I finished that that was the greatest feeling ever. No matter what, that's my gold-medal performance."

Ice skating, like everything else in life, is full of surprises. "I think this just shows, don't make predictions in skating, because who knows?" she added with a grin.

And no, she had no intention of retiring from competitive skating. "I started skating because I loved to," Sarah said. "I don't have any plans to stop. This was a great beginning to my career."

Later that afternoon, Sarah made sure she got in a long nap. Along with all the other medal winners in figure skating, she would be doing a nationally broadcast exhibition show that night. Sarah had prepared her two routines a long time before. One of them, to the song "You'll Never

Walk Alone," had originally been dedicated to the memory of fellow Olympic athletes. In 1961 a plane carrying the entire U.S. figure skating team crashed on the way to the World Championships. An entire generation of figure skaters and coaches was lost.

After the tragedy of September 11, Sarah's tribute took on a larger meaning. Now when she lay a memorial wreath on the ice, it would be for the World Trade Center victims, too. She first performed the routine at Madison Square Garden on October 5, 2001. Her taped message said:

"I am a proud American and a proud New Yorker. I am sixteen years old, and I still want to believe that our planet is big enough for everyone. My name is Sarah Hughes. I skate today in honor of those who lost their lives in 1961 in pursuit of a dream, and the thousands of innocent lives lost on September 11."

Sarah took her new position as reigning Olympic gold medalist very seriously. "There's a lot of responsibility that comes with [the gold medal]," she said. "I have a responsibility to represent my country well and a responsibility to represent the skating community well." She was already taking on the challenge.

The next week and a half rushed by in a blur of excitement. Sarah actually got to hang out with *NSYNC at an Olympic concert. "A lifelong dream!" she squealed. She presented a music award at the Grammys, where she met The Backstreet Boys, Britney Spears, and Train. (And during the ceremonies, she sat next to Janet Jackson!) And she made those guest appearances on *Saturday Night Live*, *The Tonight Show with Jay Leno* and *The Rosie O'Donnell Show*.

As Olympic gold medalist, Sarah would probably receive lots of offers to make commercials and endorse products. All that could wait. But there was one offer she couldn't refuse—to have her picture on a Wheaties cereal box! Since the 1930s, the "breakfast of champions" boxes had featured such famous athletes as Babe Ruth, Kristi Yamaguchi, and Michael Jordan. Sarah was so thrilled. She'd been collecting Wheaties boxes since she was a little girl! (Her favorites were Tiger Woods and the women's gymnastic team from the 1996 Atlanta Summer Games.) Now she'd be the one encouraging kids to eat their Wheaties.

Cool!

Not to mention ringing the opening bell at the New York Stock Exchange and receiving the key to New York City from Mayor Michael Bloomberg. The mayor was amazed at how much Sarah had achieved. "It's hard to describe the fire in the belly you have to have to compete at the level that Sarah Hughes competes," he said during the presentation. "It's something that the rest of us don't have."

It was all unbelievably great. But after a few weeks on the road, Sarah was beginning to miss ordinary life. She missed quality time with friends. She wanted to get back to her history class and start studying for the SATs. She wanted to visit her neighborhood deli, the Deli on the Green, where the owners had named her usual sandwich after her, now calling it a Golden Sarah Hughes sandwich. It had turkey, Swiss cheese, lettuce, tomatoes and, of course, a golden roll. Yes, it was definitely time to go home.

And back to school! On March 6, Sarah walked into her high school for the first time since the Olympics. She made her advanced placement history class and had a conference with her English teacher. Then, as always, she left before noon—to take the long trip to New Jersey and the Ice House. Some things never changed!

A few days later, Sarah marched down "Sarah Hughes Way" in her own parade. The parade ended at her high school, where fellow class-mates had hung a banner, WELCOME HOME SARAH.

Everyone wanted to congratulate their home-town hero, from Sarah's own friends to New York politicians. Speaking on the steps of the school, New York Senator Hillary Clinton said that Sarah's victory was "a wonderful boost to people all over the country and especially to New Yorkers." Senator Chuck Schumer said that "anyone who wants to look for a role model, whether you be five or fifty-five, can look to Sarah Hughes."

Best of all, the State of New York gave Sarah a brand-new set of license plates. They said TRPL TRPL, in honor of her two record-breaking triple combinations in the long pro-gram. Sarah could hardly wait to learn how to drive. Now she had her own custom license plates!

At the end of the ceremony, Sarah got up to speak. Her speech was sincere and from the heart.

First she told everyone in Great Neck how much she appreciated their love and support. She was surprised to see all the signs in shop windows when she came home, she said. "Having a little place in your window is like having a place in your heart," she told the thousands who had come to hear her speak.

We all need support and love, she reminded the audience. It's important to "remember the people who helped get you where you are, and the ones who will help you get where you're going."

Sarah's own helpers were sharing the podium with her. First there was her coach, Robin Wagner, who on those long trips to New Jersey had taught her about classical music, art, sportsmanship, and life. In turn, Sarah joked, she taught Robin about "high school, pop music, and the Internet."

Then she turned to her dad, John Hughes. "I have never encountered a better person than my dad and I don't think I ever will," Sarah said. He had taught her that "nothing is worthwhile if you don't have someone you love to share it with."

None of this, Sarah emphasized, would have been possible without her mother. All her siblings shared their mother's spirit, she said, but none of them had her incredible energy. Particularly, she added, "I want to thank my mom for making me do the dishes and my own laundry."

Finally, she encouraged everyone to follow their dreams, the way she did. "I didn't skate for fame," Sarah said. "I've learned that having insincere motivations in life doesn't take you anywhere. I skated with my heart."

Sarah Hughes has already achieved the dream she had when she was eight years old. But she has other dreams, too. Like every other sixteen-year-old, she wants to go to college. She wants to take her SATs and do well on them—in the high 1500s!

She really, really wants to get her driver's license.

When she graduates from college, maybe it will be on to law school—or medical school. Maybe she'll become a professional ice skater, or a professional politician, or even a columnist for *The New York Times*. It's too early to tell. But it's clear that the drive, intelligence, and winning spirit that earned her a gold medal at the Olympics will take her very far indeed.

This is only the beginning of her career, Sarah says. It's only the beginning of her life.

Anything is possible.

Sarah Hughes Profile

BORN: May 2, 1985, Great Neck, NY
HEIGHT: 5' 5"
HOME CLUB: Skating Club of New York
HOMETOWN: Great Neck, New York
TRAINING SITE: The Ice House, Hackensack, New Jersey
HIGH SCHOOL: Great Neck North High School
COACH: Robin Wagner
CHOREOGRAPHER: Robin Wagner

Sarah Hughes
Competitive History

Salt Lake City Olympics—1st
U.S. Championships—3rd
World Championships—3rd
U.S. Championships—2nd
World Championships—5th
U.S. Championships—3rd
World Championships—7th
U.S. Championships—4th
World Junior Championships—2nd
U.S. Championships, Junior—1st
Eastern Sectional, Junior—1st
North Atlantic Regional, Junior—1st
1997 Eastern Sectional, Novice—6th
North Atlantic Regional, Novice—1st
1996 Eastern Sectional, Novice—10th
1996 North Atlantic Regional, Novice—3rd

SOURCE: U.S. Figure Skating Association

Ladies' Olympic Gold Medal Winners, Figure Skating

1908	London, GBR	Madge Syers (GBR)
1920	Antwerp, BEL	Magda Julin-Mauroy (SWE)
1924	Chamonix, FRA	Herma Plank-Szabo (AUT)
1928	St. Moritz, SWI	Sonja Henie (NOR)
1932	Lake Placid, USA	Sonja Henie (NOR)
1936	Garmisch, GER	Sonja Henie (NOR)
1940, 1944		Olympics not held
1948	St. Moritz, SWI	Barbara Ann Scott (CAN)
1952	Oslo, NOR	Jeannette Altwegg (GBR)
1956	Cortina, ITA	Tenley Albright (USA)
1960	Squaw Valley, USA	Carol Heiss (USA)
1964	Innsbruck, AUT	Sjouke Dijkstra (HOL)
1968	Grenoble, FRA	Peggy Fleming (USA)
1972	Sapporo, JPN	Beatrix Schuba (AUT)
1976	Innsbruck, AUT	Dorothy Hamill (USA)
1980	Lake Placid, USA	Anett Poetzsch (GDR)
1984	Sarajevo, YUG	Katarina Witt (GDR)
1988	Calgary, CAN	Katarina Witt (GDR)
1992	Albertville, FRA	Kristi Yamaguchi (USA)
1994	Lillehammer, NOR	Oksana Baiul (UKR)
1998	Nagano, JPN	Tara Lipinski (USA)
2002	Salt Lake City, USA	Sarah Hughes (USA)

Photo Credits